Snap books®

STAR BIOGRAPHIES

Justin Bieber

by Mari Bolte

Highlands Elementary School

CAPSTONE PRESS
a capstone imprint

Snap Books are published by Capstone Press,
1710 Roe Crest Drive, North Mankato, Minnesota 56003.
www.capstonepub.com

Library of Congress Cataloging-in-Publication Data
Bolte, Mari.
    Justin Bieber / by Mari Bolte.
    p. cm.—(Snap books. Star biographies)
    Summary: "Describes the life of Justin Bieber, including personal life
and music career"—Provided by publisher.
    Includes bibliographical references and index.
    ISBN 978-1-4296-8665-5 (library binding)
    ISBN 978-1-4296-9456-8 (pbk.)
    ISBN 978-1-62065-351-7 (ebook PDF)
    1. Bieber, Justin, 1994– —Juvenile literature. 2. Singers—Canada—Biography—Juvenile literature. I. Title.
ML3930.B54B66 2013
782.42164092—dc23 [B]   2012001001

Editors: Brenda Haugen and Megan Peterson
Designer: Bobbie Nuytten
Media Researcher: Marcie Spence
Production Specialist: Kathy McColley

Photo Credits:
Alamy: Marco Secchi, 7, ZUMA Wire Service, 28; AP Images: Evans Ward/Nickelodeon, 11; Capstone, 12, 15;
Corbis: Frank Trapper, 5, John Ewing/Retna Ltd., 9, Raymond Hagans/Retna Ltd., 16, WWD/Conde Nast, 24; Getty
Images: Alberto E. Rodriguez, 6, Anthony Randell/ABC, 13, Ethan Miller/ABC, 19, FilmMagic, 14, 21, Kevin Winter/
NBCUniversal, cover, Peter Kramer/NBC/NBCU Photo Bank, 29, WireImage, 27; Newscom: Splash News, 25, STS/
Wenn.com, 22

Essential content terms are **bold** and are defined at the bottom of the page where they first appear.

Printed in the United States of America in North Mankato, Minnesota.
0062013   007367R

Table of Contents

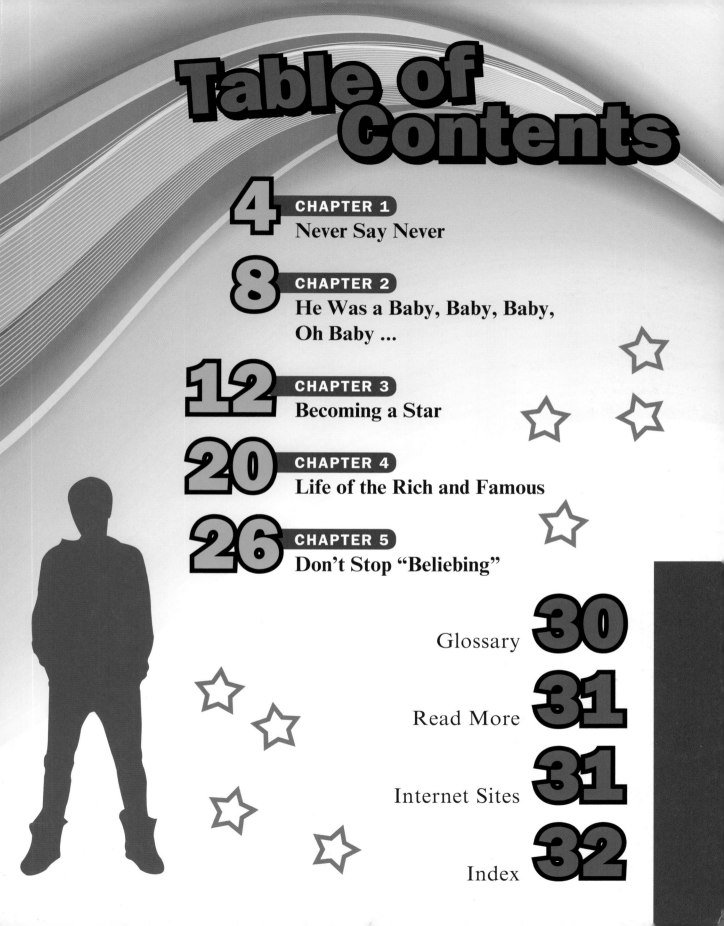

CHAPTER 1

Never Say Never

On February 8, 2011, the world saw purple. That day the 3-D **biopic** film *Justin Bieber: Never Say Never* **premiered** in Los Angeles, California. More than 1,000 screaming fans crowded together outside the Nokia Theater. Lines of fans wrapped around the block. They had been standing outside for hours but didn't seem to mind.

"I've got Bieber Fever!" one girl called to one of the many cameras capturing the event. She and many of the fans wore purple, Justin's favorite color, and held grape-colored glow sticks. The traditionally red carpet was purple. Even the 3-D glasses needed to watch the movie had violet rims.

"I'm so happy I have such amazing fans. Tonight isn't even about me. It's about spreading the message that anything is possible."
—Justin at the premiere of *Never Say Never*.

biopic—a movie about someone's life
premiere—to have a first public showing of a film

Justin wore a purple Dolce & Gabbana velvet tuxedo jacket to the premiere of his movie.

The cheering fans outside the theater weren't the only ones who came to see Justin. Teen celebs such as Selena Gomez, Jaden and Willow Smith, and Miley Cyrus walked the purple carpet. They were followed by older stars, including P. Diddy, Usher, and Jane Lynch.

Justin's movie was released in theaters worldwide three days later. In its first weekend, *Justin Bieber: Never Say Never* made nearly $30 million. As of May 2011, it earned nearly $100 million worldwide.

But Justin Bieber wasn't always a star. He had an ordinary childhood that began in a small city in Ontario, Canada.

Justin met with his fans at the premiere of *Never Say Never.*

The Bieber Cut

Justin's hair is almost as famous as his voice. His windswept bangs rocked the fashion world. Girls fell in love with the shaggy, eye-covering hair. Some salons began charging as much as $150 for the Bieber cut!

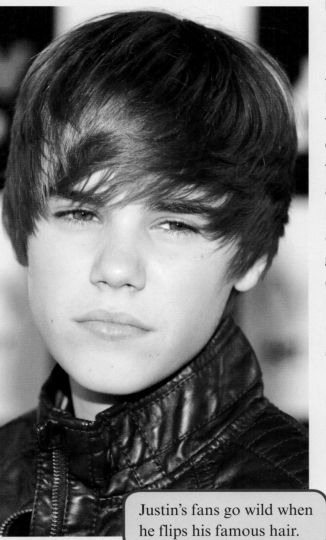

Justin's fans go wild when he flips his famous hair.

But in February 2011, Justin decided it was time for a hairstyle change. He cut off his famous locks! But the trimmings didn't go into the trash. He put them in a box, signed his name, and presented them to Ellen DeGeneres on her talk show. He asked her to sell them and to give the proceeds to her favorite charity. Justin's hair sold for $40,668 on eBay. Ellen gave the money to the Gentle Barn, an animal **rehabilitation** facility.

Justin didn't stay away from his trademark look for long. Fans were thrilled when he dyed his hair dark brown and brought back "The Bieber" in 2012.

rehabilitation—therapy that helps animals recover their health or abilities

He Was a Baby, Baby, Baby, Oh Baby ...

Justin Drew Bieber was born March 1, 1994, in London, Ontario. His parents, Jeremy Bieber and Pattie Mallette, split up when Justin was 10 months old. Pattie worked hard to support her son, but money was tight. Pattie and Justin lived in low-income housing in nearby Stratford. Justin also had a room at his grandparents' house.

From an early age, Justin was interested in music. His mom bought him his first drum set when he was 2. "He would bang on things in time to music," she has said in interviews. Justin also taught himself how to play the piano and the guitar. At first he used a right-handed guitar, but he found it hard to learn because he was left-handed. His mom bought him a left-handed guitar for his birthday. When he started middle school, he also learned to play the trumpet.

Justin learned to play the guitar at age 8.

"[My mom] loved pop music and played the radio loud when we were in the car. At home, she'd crank her stereo listening to Boyz II Men or Michael Jackson. I'd wail on whatever was handy—pots and pans, plastic bowls, tables and chairs—with whatever else was handy. Like a spoon or the phone or my fists."

—Justin on his early love of music, from his book *First Step 2 Forever: My Story.*

When Justin was 12, he entered a singing competition in Stratford called the Stratford Star. He sang songs by Ne-Yo, Matchbox Twenty, and Alicia Keys in a series of elimination rounds. Justin took third place in the final round. Justin and his mom posted videos of him in the competition on YouTube for Justin's family and friends to see. Other people began watching. Soon Justin had hundreds of followers. Pattie and Justin continued posting videos as Justin learned more songs.

Discovery

In 2007 record **executive** Scooter Braun came across one of Justin's videos. He tracked down Justin's mom. Although hesitant at first, Pattie eventually let Justin fly to Atlanta, Georgia, to record some **demo** tapes. It was both Justin's and Pattie's first time on an airplane.

In Atlanta Justin met rhythm and blues singer Usher. Justin's personality and his singing abilities won Usher over. Justin was signed to the record label Raymond Braun Media Group, a company founded by Scooter and Usher. Later Justin also signed with Island Def Jam Music Group.

With his music career taking off, Justin and Pattie decided to move to Atlanta. Scooter became Justin's manager. Justin began working with a vocal coach. He was also homeschooled. He missed regular school but enjoyed playing pranks on his tutor.

executive—a person who manages or directs
demo—a recording made to show off a new performer

Singer Usher taught Justin about the music business.

"I had to move to Atlanta, away from all my friends and family. It was pretty amazing [that] my mom left everything she knew also to come and support me."
—Justin in an interview with *E!*

Becoming a Star

In summer 2009 Justin's first **single**, "One Time," was released. It reached number 12 on the Canadian Hot 100 and number 17 on the Billboard Hot 100 singles charts. The song went platinum in the United States, selling more than 1 million copies.

Justin's first album, *My World*, was released in November. The album went platinum in the United States. Justin became the first artist to have seven songs from a **debut** album reach the Billboard Hot 100 singles chart. That same month he opened for country star Taylor Swift at a concert in London, England.

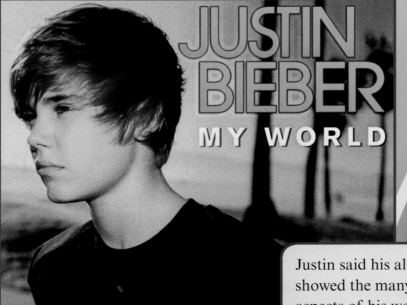

Justin said his album showed the many aspects of his world.

In November 2009 Justin performed songs from *My World* on *Good Morning America*.

Justin went on a mini tour to promote *My World*. He performed on TV shows across the country, singing on *The Today Show*, *The Ellen DeGeneres Show*, and *Good Morning America*. Tickets to see him at these appearances sold out immediately.

single—one song released to the public
debut—a first showing

In December Justin performed Stevie Wonder's song "Someday at Christmas" for President Barack Obama and his family in Washington, D.C. He also performed on *Dick Clark's New Year's Rockin' Eve with Ryan Seacrest*.

In January 2010 Justin attended the Grammy Awards. He looked sharp in a black vest and gray button-down shirt. He was in awe as he met celebrities such as LL Cool J and Adam Sandler. He even got to meet his star crush, Beyoncé! That night he stood next to Ke$ha onstage. They asked viewers to vote for their favorite Bon Jovi song to be played live on the show.

While presenting with Ke$ha, Justin flubbed his lines! He said "Beyoncé" instead of "Bon Jovi."

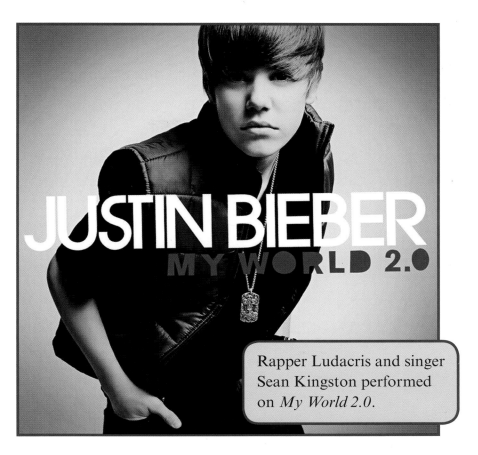

Rapper Ludacris and singer Sean Kingston performed on *My World 2.0*.

That same month the first single from his upcoming album, *My World 2.0*, was released. Justin cowrote the entire album, including the single "Baby," which was an instant hit. The YouTube video for the song became the most-viewed video of all time, with more than 720 million hits.

My World 2.0 was released in March 2010. The album reached the number-one spot on the Billboard 200 albums chart. Justin became the youngest male **solo artist** to reach that spot since Stevie Wonder in 1963.

solo artist—a musician who is the star performer of a band

The My World Tour

Justin kicked off the My World Tour on June 23, 2010, in Hartford, Connecticut. When the popular tour headed to Europe, the two Ireland shows sold out their 28,000 tickets in 10 minutes. The first show scheduled for Melbourne, Australia, sold out in minutes. Supporting acts on the tour included Sean Kingston and Jessica Jarrell. Usher, Miley Cyrus, and Jaden Smith made surprise appearances. Justin didn't just sing and dance on tour. He also played the piano and guitar for a few of his songs.

To start each show of his My World Tour, Justin appeared in a giant metal globe.

The My World Tour took Justin across the United States, Canada, Europe, Asia, Australia, and South America. While in the Philippines, Justin refused to miss a concert when he became ill. Even though he had to run backstage to get sick, he still finished his show. He didn't want to disappoint his fans.

Justin's tour dates in May 2011 took him to Japan. The country had been hit by a huge **tsunami** and earthquake just a few months earlier. He decided the show must go on. Justin met victims affected by the disaster.

Life on the Road

Touring wasn't only about performing for Justin. He also had to study hard. Every day he worked with a tutor for three hours. But he still found time to have fun. Justin played video games on his tour bus. He scooted around on a Segway during concert rehearsals.

"Things can get better and things will get better. There can only be good times to come from this and my prayers go out to all of your families."

—Justin speaking to the victims of the 2011 tsunami in Japan.

tsunami—a large, destructive wave caused by an underwater earthquake

Awards

In November 2010 Justin released *My Worlds Acoustic*. The album had nine acoustic versions of Justin's hits from *My World* and *My World 2.0*, as well as one new song. It reached number seven on the Billboard 200 albums chart, giving Justin his third top-10 album.

In December Justin was **nominated** for Grammy awards in the Best New Artist and Best Pop Vocal Album categories. The awards show was in February 2011. Justin walked the red carpet in a white velvet Dolce & Gabbana three-piece tuxedo. A black bow tie, black pocket square, and white sneakers set off the stylish outfit. He was a presenter and also performed with Jaden Smith and Usher to a screaming crowd. Although Justin didn't win an award, he knew that this wouldn't be his last nomination.

"It's all about remembering to stay calm and not worrying. I don't really get nervous. But I'm kind of nervous [tonight] because I'm performing with Usher. He's so good, and I don't want to look bad."

—Justin on his performance at the Grammys, from an interview with *E!*

acoustic—music made by instruments that aren't electric

nominate—to name someone as a candidate for an award

Justin didn't have to wait long to win a big award. A few months later, he was nominated for 11 awards at the 2011 Billboard Music Awards in Las Vegas. He won six awards, including Top New Artist and Top Pop Album for *My World 2.0*. Wearing a gold and black suit coat and black tuxedo pants, he was a well-dressed winner.

Justin was excited to win the award for Top New Artist at the 2011 Billboard Music Awards.

CHAPTER 4

Life of the Rich and Famous

Never Say Never: The Remixes came out in February 2011. It accompanied Justin's movie and was mostly made up of remixed Bieber songs. Justin and Jaden Smith **collaborated** on the album's title song, "Never Say Never." It became the theme song to Jaden's new movie, *The Karate Kid*. The album sold more than 165,000 copies its first week. It also reached number one on the Billboard 200 albums chart.

After the release of *Never Say Never*, Justin's stardom reached a whole new level. He was invited to play in the 2011 NBA All-Star Celebrity Game at the Los Angeles Convention Center. His teammates included celebs Zachary Levi and Rob Kardashian. Scoring eight points and getting four assists and two rebounds, Justin was voted the game's MVP.

collaborate—to work together to do something

Justin, shown here with rapper Common, showed off his basketball skills at the 2011 NBA All-Star Celebrity Game.

"It still feels like a dream. I'm starting to realize this is crazy. I used to listen to the radio and hear other people, and now I listen to it and hear myself. It's crazy."
—Justin on his fame, from an interview with *Good Morning America.*

The Ups and Downs of Fame

Justin soon learned that being famous comes with a price. **Paparazzi** follow Justin wherever he goes. Every move he makes is discussed in magazines, on TV, and on the Internet. People want to know everything about him—including his personal life. When Justin started dating celeb Selena Gomez, fans expressed their opinions, both good and bad.

Of course being famous does have its perks. In 2011 Justin took the number-three slot on Forbes' Celebrity 100 List, earning $53 million the year before. He was right behind Lady Gaga and Oprah. He was the youngest celeb on the list. Justin's concerts bring in $600,000 a night alone. Justin's fame allows him to travel the world and meet other celebs.

Justin and Selena Gomez dodged cameras after leaving a restaurant in Los Angeles.

> "#10MillionBeliebers I love u ... changing my life everyday. I'm from a town of 30,000 ... so u guys are 333 times my town! CRAZY! #NeverSayNever."
> —Justin tweeting on reaching 10 million Twitter followers in May 2011.

How Many Friends?

Justin makes himself known using social media. He has more than 18 million Twitter followers, 1.4 million YouTube subscribers, and more than 40 million Facebook fans. Tweets related to Justin account for at least 3 percent of Twitter's overall traffic. He receives at least 60 @-replies per second right after tweeting. It has been said that he is more **influential** in the social networking world than Katy Perry and President Barack Obama.

In 2011 Google chose Justin as their spokesperson. They hoped he could bring new users to the Google Chrome web browser. They also made a commercial showing Justin using Google Chrome to upload his videos. By February 2012 the commercial had been viewed more than 2.5 million times on YouTube.

paparazzi—aggressive photographers who take pictures of celebrities for sale to magazines
influential—having an effect on someone

Justin's mom, Pattie, is supportive of her son's career. She travels with him all the time and is at almost every concert. She also keeps his spending in line. Justin gets an allowance of $50 a day, and once it's gone, it's gone. One big-ticket item he bought himself was a MacBook Pro computer. Justin also loves cars. He has a Range Rover, a 16th birthday present from Usher. He has also been spotted driving his Batman-themed Cadillac CTS-V.

Justin also likes to use his fame to help others. When he turned 17, he asked people to give $17 to *My*Charity: Water, rather than buy him gifts. The charity helps people in developing countries get access to clean water. Justin's fans donated more than $40,000.

Of course that doesn't mean Justin didn't do anything on his big day. Justin spent the morning with his family. That evening he and girlfriend Selena Gomez were spotted at Maggiano's Little Italy restaurant in Los Angeles.

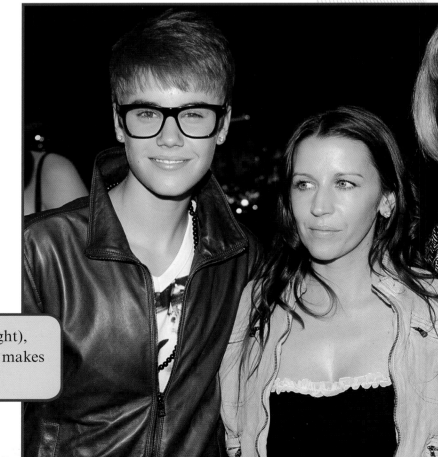

Justin's mom, Pattie (right), supports his career and makes sure he stays grounded.

Justin doesn't just love Italian food. In June he and Selena were seen in Justin's hometown in Ontario. They visited with Justin's family over burgers and wings. The couple stopped at Scooper's Ice Cream Treats. Justin ordered a double raspberry frozen yogurt and convinced Selena to try the store's Rolo flavor. Some of Justin's other favorite foods include Sour Patch Kids, ketchup-flavored potato chips, and Swedish Fish candy. He also loves spaghetti Bolognese and his grandma's cherry cheesecake.

Happy 18th Birthday, Justin!

On March 1, 2012, Justin turned 18. He appeared on *The Ellen DeGeneres Show,* where his manager Scooter Braun presented him with a car. But not just any car—a Fisker Karma. The car is an electric luxury sedan with a solar-powered roof. The car usually sells for more than $100,000. Glass flakes in the paint make the car shine like a diamond. It goes from 0 to 60 miles (97 kilometers) per hour in 6.3 seconds or less.

CHAPTER 5

Don't Stop "Beliebing"

Although Justin's life changed dramatically once he became famous, he still wants a normal life. He loves watching his favorite TV show, *Smallville*. He sets aside one day a week to relax. He rides skateboard and plays basketball, hockey, and golf in his free time

Family has always been important to Justin. When he's not touring, he's spending time with those closest to him. Even though he wasn't raised by his dad, the Bieber boys still do things together. Justin and Jeremy have been spotted surfing and shooting hoops. Justin also loves playing with his two half siblings, Jaxon and Jazmyn.

In 2011 Justin brought his sister, Jazmyn, to the Canadian TV show *New.Music.Live.*

Justin also enjoys hanging out with his friends. In December 2011 he took friends Alfredo Flores and Jaden Smith to Disney World and Universal Studios in Orlando, Florida. The friends drank butterbeer at the Wizarding World of Harry Potter. They also took pictures with childhood icons, including Woody from *Toy Story* and Goofy.

Future Plans

Although Justin plans on focusing mostly on his music career, he also hopes to do a little acting. In April 2011 it was announced that he would star alongside Mark Wahlberg in a movie about basketball. Wahlberg saw Justin play at the NBA All-Star Game and was impressed. Justin has already guest starred on the hit TV show *CSI*.

Justin says he might go to college one day. Since he likes to write, an English degree might be a possibility. The budding author's first book, a **memoir** called *First Step 2 Forever: My Story*, was released in 2010. He is at work on a second memoir.

In 2010 Justin signed copies of his book at a Barnes & Noble in Hollywood, California.

memoir—a narrative composed from personal experience

Justin's career kept him busy in the winter of 2011–2012. He signed Canadian pop singer Carly Rae Jepsen to his label, Schoolboy Records. Justin runs the label with Scooter. Justin also released his first Christmas album, *Under the Mistletoe*. He paired his voice with Busta Rhymes, Mariah Carey, The Band Perry, Usher, and Boyz II Men.

The album debuted at number one on the Billboard 200 albums chart, selling 210,000 copies its first week. *Under the Mistletoe* was the first holiday song collection by a male artist to hold that spot. With a new album, *Believe*, due out in 2012, who knows what new records Justin might break?

Justin, shown here signing autographs at *The Today Show* in 2011, credits his fans with his success.

Glossary

acoustic (uh-KOOS-tik)—music made by instruments that aren't electric

biopic (BYE-oh-pik)—a movie about someone's life

collaborate (kuh-LAB-uh-rate)—to work together to do something

debut (day-BYOO)—a first showing

demo (DEM-oh)—a recording made to show off a new performer or piece of music

executive (ig-ZE-kyuh-tiv)—a person who manages or directs

influential (in-floo-EN-chuhl)—having an effect on someone or something

memoir (MEM-wohr)—a narrative composed from personal experience

nominate (NOM-uh-nate)—to name someone as a candidate for an award

paparazzi (pah-puh-RAHT-see)—aggressive photographers who take pictures of celebrities for sale to magazines or newspapers

premiere (PRUH-meer)—to have a first public performance of a film, play, or work of music or dance

rehabilitation (ree-huh-bil-uh-TAY-shun)—therapy that helps animals recover their health or abilities

single (SING-guhl)—one song released to the public

solo artist (SOH-loh AR-tist)—a musician who is the star performer of a band; solo artists usually perform alone or with backup musicians

tsunami (tsoo-NAH-mee)—a large, destructive wave caused by an underwater earthquake

Read More

Azzarelli, Ally. *Justin Bieber: Teen Music Superstar*. Hot Celebrity Biographies. Berkeley Heights, N.J.: Enslow Publishers, 2012.

Brooks, Riley. *Justin Bieber: His World.* New York: Scholastic, 2010.

Tracy, Kathleen. *Justin Bieber*. A Robbie Reader. Hockessin, Del.: Mitchell Lane, 2011.

Yasuda, Anita. *Justin Bieber*. Remarkable People. New York: AV2 by Weigl, 2012.

Internet Sites

FactHound offers a safe, fun way to find Internet sites related to this book. All of the sites on FactHound have been researched by our staff.

Here's all you do:

Visit *www.facthound.com*

Type in this code: 9781429686655

 Check out projects, games and lots more at
www.capstonekids.com

Index